Office Dogs

The Manual

STEPHANIE ROUSSEAU

Hubble & Hattie

The Hubble & Hattie imprint was launched in 2009 and is named in memory of two very special Westies owned by Veloce's proprietors. Since the first book, many more have been added to the list, all with the same underlying objective: to be of real benefit to the species they cover, at the same time promoting compassion, understanding and respect between all animals (including human ones!)

Hubble & Hattie is the home of a range of books that cover all-things animal, produced to the same high quality of content and presentation as our motoring books, and offering the same great value for money.

More great Hubble & Hattie books!

Among the Wolves: Memoirs of a wolf handler (Shelbourne)
Animal Grief: How animals mourn (Alderton)
Babies, kids and dogs – creating a safe and harmonious relationship (Fallon & Davenport)
Because this is our home ... the story of a cat's progress (Bowes)
Bonds – Capturing the special relationship that dogs share with their people (Cukuraite & Pais)
Camper vans, ex-pats & Spanish Hounds: from road trip to rescue – the strays of Spain (Coates & Morris)
Canine aggression – how kindness and compassion saved Calgacus (McLennan)
Cat and Dog Health, The Complete Book of (Hansen)
Cat Speak: recognising & understanding behaviour (Rauth-Widmann)
Charlie – The dog who came in from the wild (Tenzin-Dolma)
Clever dog! Life lessons from the world's most successful animal (O'Meara)
Complete Dog Massage Manual, The – Gentle Dog Care (Robertson)
Confessions of a veterinary nurse: paws, claws and puppy dog tails (Ison)
Detector Dog – A Talking Dogs Scentwork Manual (Mackinnon)
Dieting with my dog: one busy life, two full figures ... and unconditional love (Frezon)
Dinner with Rover: delicious, nutritious meals for you and your dog to share (Paton-Ayre)
Dog Cookies: healthy, allergen-free treat recipes for your dog (Schöps)
Dog-friendly gardening: creating a safe haven for you and your dog (Bush)
Dog Games – stimulating play to entertain your dog and you (Blenski)
Dog Relax – relaxed dogs, relaxed owners (Pilguj)
Dog Speak: recognising & understanding behaviour (Blenski)
Dogs just wanna have Fun! Picture this: dogs at play (Murphy)
Dogs on Wheels: travelling with your canine companion (Mort)
Emergency First Aid for dogs: at home and away Revised Edition (Bucksch)
Exercising your puppy: a gentle & natural approach – Gentle Dog Care (Robertson & Pope)
For the love of Scout: promises to a small dog (Ison)
Fun and Games for Cats (Seidl)
Gods, ghosts, and black dogs – the fascinating folklore and mythology of dogs (Coren)
Helping minds meet – skills for a better life with your dog (Zulch & Mills)
Home alone – and happy! Essential life skills for preventing separation anxiety in dogs and puppies (Mallatratt)
Know Your Dog – The guide to a beautiful relationship (Birmelin)
Letting in the dog: opening hearts and minds to a deeper understanding (Blocker)
Life skills for puppies – laying the foundation for a loving, lasting relationship (Zuch & Mills)
Lily: One in a million! A miracle of survival (Hamilton)
Living with an Older Dog – Gentle Dog Care (Alderton & Hall)
Miaow! Cats really are nicer than people! (Moore)
Mike&Scrabble – A guide to training your new Human (Dicks & Scrabble)
Mike&Scrabble Too – Further tips on training your Human (Dicks & Scrabble)
My cat has arthritis – but lives life to the full! (Carrick)
My dog has arthritis – but lives life to the full! (Carrick)
My dog has cruciate ligament injury – but lives life to the full! (Haüsler & Friedrich)
My dog has epilepsy – but lives life to the full! (Carrick)
My dog has hip dysplasia – but lives life to the full! (Haüsler & Friedrich)
My dog is blind – but lives life to the full! (Horsky)
My dog is deaf – but lives life to the full! (Willms)
My Dog, my Friend: heart-warming tales of canine companionship from celebrities and other extraordinary people (Gordon)
Office Dogs: The Manual (Rousseau)
One Minute Cat Manager: sixty seconds to feline Shangri-la (Young)
Ollie and Nina and ... daft doggy doings! (Sullivan)
No walks? No worries! Maintaining wellbeing in dogs on restricted exercise (Ryan & Zulch)
Partners – Everyday working dogs being heroes every day (Walton)
Puppy called Wolfie – a passion for free will teaching (Gregory)
Smellorama – nose games for dogs (Theby)
Supposedly enlightened person's guide to raising a dog (Young & Tenzin-Dolma)
Swim to recovery: canine hydrotherapy healing – Gentle Dog Care (Wong)
Tale of two horses – a passion for free will teaching (Gregory)
Tara – the terrier who sailed around the world (Forrester)
Truth about Wolves and Dogs, The: dispelling the myths of dog training (Shelbourne)
Unleashing the healing power of animals: True stories about therapy animals – and what they do for us (Preece-Kelly)
Waggy Tails & Wheelchairs (Epp)
Walking the dog: motorway walks for drivers & dogs revised edition (Rees)
When man meets dog – what a difference a dog makes (Blazina)
Wildlife photography from the edge (Williams)
Winston ... the dog who changed my life (Klute)
Wonderful walks from dog-friendly campsites throughout the UK (Chelmicka)
Worzel Wooface: For the love of Worzel (Pickles)
Worzel Wooface: The quite very actual adventures of (Pickles)
Worzel Wooface: The quite very actual Terribibble Twos (Pickles)
Worzel Wooface: Three quite very actual cheers for (Pickles)
You and Your Border Terrier – The Essential Guide (Alderton)
You and Your Cockapoo – The Essential Guide (Alderton)
Your dog and you – understanding the canine psyche (Garratt)

Hubble & Hattie Kids!

Fierce Grey Mouse (Bourgonje)
Indigo Warrios: The Adventure Begins! (Moore)
Lucky, Lucky Leaf, The: A Horace & Nim story (Bourgonje & Hoskins)
Little house that didn't have a home, The (Sullivan & Burke)
Lily and the Little Lost Doggie, The Adventures of (Hamilton)
Wandering Wildebeest, The (Coleman & Slater)
Worzel goes for a walk! Will you come too? (Pickles & Bourgonje)
Worzel says hello! Will you be my friend? (Pickles & Bourgonje)

First published in March 2019 by Veloce Publishing Limited, Veloce House, Parkway Farm Business Park, Middle Farm Way, Poundbury, Dorchester, Dorset, DT1 3AR, England. Tel 01305 260068/fax 01305 250479/e-mail info@hubbleandhattie.com/web www.hubbleandhattie.com. ISBN: 978-1-787113-81-7 UPC: 6-36847-01381-3 Readers with ideas for books about animals, or animal-related topics, are invited to write to the editorial director of Veloce Publishing at the above address. British Library Cataloguing in Publication Data – A catalogue record for this book is available from the British Library. Typesetting, design and page make-up all by Veloce Publishing Ltd on Apple Mac. Printed and bound in India by Replika Press PTY

Contents

Dedication & Acknowledgements

Dedicated to the memory of Alfie
(1 May 2004-21 December 2017)

I wasn't lying you know: you really were the best boy

My thanks go first and foremost to Turid Rugaas: this book started out as a final project for her International Dog Trainer's Education (IDTE), and is strongly informed by her teachings and methodologies.

My thanks also to Karen and Alan Webb, without whom there would not have been an IDTE in the UK, and to Winkie Spiers whose willingness to take extra passengers greatly facilitated mine and Fia's attendance!

I would also like to express my gratitude to Tom, who read and re-read drafts, and patiently offered constructive criticism and unwavering support; to Erik for his legal input, and to my mum for all of her help and encouragement through the years.

Last, but by no means least, to all of the people who shared their experiences of working alongside dogs in the workplace. Without your help, there would be a lot less to say!

Stephanie Rousseau

About the author

Steph has always been passionate about dogs, and, wherever she went as a child, acquired canine pals. When she went missing as a toddler, she was subsequently found, some distance away, sitting under a hedge with the neighbour's dog! The draw to canids continued into adulthood, but it was in 2010, when Steph adopted a retired ex-racing Greyhound called Alfie, that a career working with dogs became a consideration. Alfie's array of challenging behaviours led Steph into the world of PDTE (Pet Dog Trainers of Europe) dog trainers, and to a natural way of dog training that was far from the obedience ring she had always imagined when anyone mentioned dog training.

She finally set up a dog training and behaviour business in London in 2014, where she worked with hundreds of dogs, from puppies to adults with serious behavioural issues. She became a member of the PDTE in 2015, completed Turid Rugaas' International Dog Trainer's Education in 2016/2017, and it was as a final project for that course that this book had its humble beginnings. Steph's inspiration came from a number of clients she had met who were struggling with their dogs' behaviour in the work environment. This led her to consider what simple steps could be put in place to ensure that this increasingly popular trend could work for both the dogs involved and their humans.

Steph relocated to her hometown of Dublin in 2017, where she lives with her two dogs: Fia, the most beautiful rescue Greyhound, and Ferdia, a rather handsome ex-laboratory Beagle cross. Since beginning work on this book, her focus on office dogs has increased. Alongside her training and behaviour work, Steph visits workplaces to help workers learn more about their dogs, and how office life can be tweaked to be as stress-free as possible for them, as well as offering advice and help to businesses that are considering becoming dog-friendly.

Foreword

by Turid Rugaas

In many countries it has become quite common to enrich the working environment with the presence of a dog, so if it has occurred to you to bring your dog to work, you are not alone. Perhaps you have had some doubts about how to raise the issue with your boss or colleagues; about whether the experience will benefit your dog, and, if so, how to deal with the practicalities of bringing your dog to work? Or maybe you already bring your dog to work and wish to make the experience as positive as possible for all involved.

This book is for all of you, no matter what questions you have. The author, Stephanie Rousseau, has completed my IDTE (International Dog Trainers' Education), and has a great deal of knowledge about dogs. And, not least of all, she has a great love for dogs!

In this book, Stephanie guides you through the options you have; the problems you might encounter, and what you need to consider, taking into account both the wellbeing of the dog and the environment.

This book is a gem – full of information, inspiration and practical advice. If you have ever considered bringing your dog to work, this book will be an invaluable resource for you and your dog.

I am very happy to be able to recommend this book!

Turid Rugaas
President of the PDTE

Introduction

Taking pets to work is growing in popularity, and at the time of writing, around 8% of workplaces in the UK and US allow employees to bring their dogs to work. This includes lots of the big employers, such as Google, Facebook, Etsy, Airbnb; some of the larger pet food companies like Purina and Lily's Kitchen, as well as many smaller businesses.

Workplaces are changing, and more and more employers are looking for effective ways to improve the working environment for staff, and in some cases, to motivate them to spend more time there.

Employees are also changing. Millennials, the generation who will increasingly dominate the workforce over the coming years, are committed pet owners. Although less likely to be married or living with partners, they are more likely to have pets than any other generation, with 75% of Americans in their thirties having a dog. So, for employers,

Miss Bronte.
(Courtesy Jude Brooks)

finding ways to facilitate pet ownership has the potential to give them the edge when it comes to recruiting this demographic of workers.

Studies have illustrated a host of benefits to companies and employees of having dogs in the workplace: everything from reduced stress amongst staff and increased job satisfaction and employee retention, to the health-boosting effects that come from having pets around.

Add to that the benefits to devoted dog parents who can take their dogs to work and not worry about them being lonely at home, and of course, the benefits to the estimated 50-90% of dogs who suffer from separation anxiety, and it definitely sounds like an idea with potential!

However, whilst capitalising on the benefits of implementing a dog-friendly policy that will work for the business and its employees, we must not forget to scrutinise the advantages (and disadvantages) attached to going to work for the dogs themselves.

My experience as a dog trainer has taught me that, despite the best will in the world, humans are sometimes unaware of the fact that their dog may be experiencing stress. When I have worked with dogs who have been displaying undesirable behaviours in the work environment (and, in fact, any other environment), stress is often the root cause.

This suggests that going to work is not necessarily a universally positive experience for our dogs. I believe, however, that with a little pre-planning and a broader understanding of the situations that could cause a dog stress, most working environments and routines can be tweaked to reduce the chances of a dog becoming stressed and potentially misbehaving.

This book deals with the practicalities of preparing to take your dog to work, including selling the idea to your employer and colleagues, and some of the potential pitfalls for which you may wish to prepare. It also looks at the experience from your dog's perspective: how you can make it as stress-free as possible, some useful skills to teach your dog, and a section on dealing with some of the behavioural issues that may arise.

I hope that this book will be a useful resource to dog owners who are considering taking their dogs to work, as well as to those who already do, and would like to make the experience as stress-free and rewarding as possible for all concerned.

Starring

Pater, Lurcher, and Cookie, Labrador: software developers.
(Courtesy Lea Jochmann)

Sadie, Cockapoo, public relations.

Penny, Bull Terrier, architect.

Molly, German Shepherd, estate agent.
(Courtesy Kelly Hollis)

Huntley, Collie, service technology.
(Courtesy Jan Hugo Borg-Magnussen)

Bobby, Miniature Dachshund, marketing.

Poppy, Jug, legal services, estate planning.
(Courtesy Teressa McDonald)

Chapter 1

Laying the groundwork

Selling the idea

Thankfully, there is no shortage of evidence supporting the advantages to us of having dogs in the office. If your workplace already allows dogs, getting permission to take in your dog may simply be a case of a chat with your line manager, or filling in a form. If you need to make a case for having your dog along, here are just a few of the points you can make –

- ✔ A 2012 study found that allowing dogs in the workplace reduced stress (a major contributor to employee absenteeism, and one that's expected to rise over the coming years), and increased job satisfaction
- ✔ Another study from the same year showed that having dogs around increased cohesion and team satisfaction
- ✔ A 2002 study found that dogs being present lowered blood pressure in stressful situations
- ✔ Dogs have been found to increase social interaction and improve mood
- ✔ A dog-friendly policy can lead to enhanced recruitment
- ✔ Dogs in the workplace have been shown to improve employee retention – one study showed that staff were 53% more likely to stay with a pet-friendly company
- ✔ Another study found that two thirds of Human Resource decision-makers are asked about pet-friendly policies

✔ It's been found that allowing dogs in work increases employee productivity

And all with no financial input required from the employer! In fact, 65% of respondents to a survey in *Modern Dog* magazine said they would take a reduced salary if it meant they could take their dog to work.

Whilst making your case, it's important to consider your workplace and its priorities, as well as any concerns your employer may have, and what you can offer as mitigating factors. There are a number of potential risks and disadvantages that your employer might be concerned about, though many of these can be reduced or eliminated –

? Insurance and claims if something goes wrong, who will be responsible? Having the appropriate liability insurance as well as a signed indemnification agreement between employer and employee stipulating that the latter will ultimately assume responsibility for any liability suffered by the employer by permitting dogs in the workplace may go some way toward allaying this concern

? Does the lease allow it? Many workplaces are leased, and if the lease prohibits animals on the premises your employer could find itself in breach of its obligations. If the lease does not allow dogs in the workplace, your employer may be able to negotiate an exception

? Cultural sensitivities Some religions consider dogs unclean, and working in close proximity with them may be a problem for advocates of such religions. There are cultures that regard canines as guard dogs only, and find them threatening. Is the workplace designed in such a way that enough distance can be maintained between those who do not wish to be around dogs for whatever reason and the dogs?

? Allergies 15-30% of people with allergies are allergic to cats and dogs. Some of the allergens from dogs will linger in an area that the animal has been in even after they have left. Maintaining dog-friendly and dog-free zones may be possible for those with allergies to use. Dog-friendly zones should be clearly marked to avoid someone with allergies accidentally entering an area with allergens, even though there are no dogs present

? Health There may be concern around zoonotic diseases such as parasites. Having guidelines surrounding regular vet check-ups and vaccinations where appropriate could address this issue. Additionally, simple, basic hand hygiene can negate almost all risks

? Trip and fall hazards The dogs themselves, their leads or accessories could pose a trip hazard. Most workplaces have the potential for trip and fall

Sadie with Breffni at work.

Case study: Sadie

Sadie is a 7-month-old Cockapoo who goes to work at Host, a city centre-based PR company in Dublin, with her human, Breffni.

Breffni had wanted a dog for a while, but was concerned about leaving her home alone all day. Luckily for Breffni, when she mentioned her dilemma in passing at work, her boss told her that if she got a dog, she could bring her to the office.

In November 2017, Breffni acquired Sadie in a spur of the moment decision, and, just days later, was taking her to the office.

Breffni admits that the first couple of months were a bit tricky on the toileting front, and it took Sadie longer to grasp toilet training at work than it did at home. With the office based on the first floor, it wasn't as simple as just opening the door and letting her out.

The workforce in Host are pretty dog-friendly; the MD sometimes brings his own dog to the office, and most of the staff are pet owners. Everyone was happy to make the small changes that were required to keep the little Cockapoo (and their belongings!) safe. Wires were of particular interest to the young Sadie, so it was necessary to turn off electronic devices at the socket if she was going to be left at all. Everyone got into the habit of keeping their bags off the floor, and casualties were few. A MacBook cable met its maker, and an expensive pair of Ugg mittens had a lucky escape. Despite this, the attitude towards Sadie remains positive, with the office motto being 'it takes an office to rear a pup,' and everyone agreeing that having a dog around definitely reduces stress. They're even willing to put up with her chewing on miscellaneous animal parts, such as cows' ears, at work!

When Sadie was small she and Breffni used to travel to work by bus (in Dublin, dogs are allowed on buses at the driver's discretion). They rarely encountered any problems, however, and most of the drivers were happy to allow her on. Now she's bigger, they mostly make the journey to work on foot. At lunchtime, they go to a local park, where Sadie often meets her friend, another office dog called Phoebe.

Like most dogs, Sadie likes to be at the centre of things, and no matter what she's doing, always makes sure to join in on the daily morning meetings, which she often spends lying on someone's lap.

Breffni thinks that having dogs at work is a nice thing for a boss to accommodate, and being allowed to have Sadie with her makes her feel appreciated as a member of staff: she agrees that allowing dogs at work is an excellent staff-retention strategy!

hazards, so – as with other potential risks – having specific rules about where these items should be kept could reduce the risk

? Phobias Some employees may have a dislike or even fear of dogs. Again, maintaining dog-friendly and dog-free zones should help. Making new employees aware of the dog-friendly nature of the office at recruitment stage can avoid any surprises once they commence employment

? Behaviour A badly-behaved dog has the potential to be a source of conflict and frustration in the workplace. Ensuring dogs have the necessary skills to be in the office is important (see Chapter 5, *Useful skills*)

Policies

Policies on dogs in the workplace are surprisingly few. In a study carried out by Sophie Hall and Hannah Wright, et al, in 2017, it was found that 65.9% of people who were allowed to take their dog to work were not aware of any specific policies relating to dogs in their workplace. Of those whose workplaces did have specific policies relating to dogs, the most common criterion determining whether or not a dog was allowed at work was behaviour.

Other policies stipulated certain days or times when a dog was allowed, whilst others stated that the dog's presence was subject to spatial restrictions (keeping them in/out of certain places).

Having a well-thought-out policy in place can help ensure that everyone is clear on the rules and limitations. The case studies that follow offer insight into the type of issues other organisations have taken into consideration whilst drafting dog-friendly policies.

Policy case studies

Amazon

Amazon in Seattle has a dog-friendly policy, and on its website states that up to 500 dogs may be present at the Seattle office on any given day. Its policy for allowing dogs at work states that –

✔ The employee must have conversations with their manager as well as colleagues in their immediate work area to ensure everyone is comfortable with the dog's presence

✔ The employee then submits a registration form for their dog and provides proof of vaccination

✔ Dogs who accompany their owners to work sit with them at their desks or in their area, either on a leash or short tether, or in a penned area

Kurgo's reclaimed timber pods: these create a nice, safe place for the dogs in proximity to their owners. *(Courtesy Kurgo)*

Kurgo
At Kurgo, a pet supplies company in Massachusetts, dogs (and rats!) are also allowed in the office. Kurgo asks that employees who wish to take dogs to work sign a pet policy, that indicates all damage by and liability for the dog's actions are their responsibility, and that they'll clean up after their dog. There is also a requirement that the dogs be up-to-date with vaccinations; are toilet-trained; able to behave appropriately with new people and dogs, and, if they can't be trusted to behave well off-lead, that they be on-lead or else in an office or cubicle (Kurgo has brilliant cubicles, made from reclaimed timber from the rivers in Maine).

The company has not divided space into dog-friendly and dog-free zones, and makes it clear during the interview process that it is a dog-friendly office, and staff could well be expected to interact with dogs as part of their role, so anyone who is allergic to or uncomfortable with dogs is unlikely to want to work there.

Butternut Box
Butternut Box, a UK-based company providing a home-cooked food delivery service for dogs, operates from a dog-friendly office space. The lease requires staff who wish to bring in dogs to fill out an authorisation and release form that confirms the dogs are up-to-date with vaccinations, regularly treated for parasites, and have no recent history of infection or ringworm. With regard to behaviour, the dogs must be toilet-trained, not have bitten anyone or be aggressive, and not be destructive or excessively vocal. Their owner agrees to clean up any mess the dog makes; not to bring a sick dog to work, and to remove the dog from the premises if they become unwell or are behaving abnormally.

Further stipulations are that dogs should be on-leash or otherwise contained whilst on the premises, and are not allowed in certain areas, such as food preparation areas, rest rooms, and kitchen areas. The employee must also sign a waiver of liability for any damage, injury or loss incurred either directly or indirectly by the dog's presence.

Gaining your colleagues' support

Gaining support from colleagues is key to ensuring the dog-friendly arrangement works, especially in small businesses. It's important to ensure that people feel free to express concerns before any agreement is reached.

I carried out a short survey of one hundred people to establish their attitude to dogs in the workplace, and, overall, the response was very positive. Of those surveyed, 81% were in favour of a dog-friendly policy, and 92% of those would either be willing to change their behaviour to accommodate this policy, or were open to persuasion on this point. Interestingly, the way in which they'd be least willing to change their behaviour was in relation to noise reduction (although 90% were still either 'very willing' or 'willing' to do so), so if you have a sound-sensitive dog, and a noisy work environment, this is worth bearing in mind. The vast majority of people who were in favour of dogs in the workplace were also willing to attend training events about issues such as canine communication, making the office work for both dogs and humans, and fun and healthy activities for dogs.

Of those who were against having dogs in the workplace, the most common reason for this was that they thought the dogs would be disruptive or a distraction; others simply didn't like dogs, were allergic to them, or didn't feel the work environment was suitable for dogs. Of those who were against having dogs in the office, 20% would change their mind if there were dog-friendly and dog-free zones in the workplace so that they didn't have to interact with them. A further 30% said they 'might change their mind' if this was the case.

So, it seems the odds are actually in favour of colleagues being largely supportive of the idea. Where there is an objection, there's a good chance that simple guidelines or minor compromise (such as dog-free areas) may be sufficient to allay concerns. Chat to colleagues to establish what would make a dog-friendly arrangement acceptable.

Ensuring your colleagues know the reality of having a dog in the office

The idea of having a dog in the office – and the reality of having a dog in the office – can be two very different things, and this can be particularly true in the case of puppies or recent rescues who may not yet have developed appropriate skills. If you are hoping to take your dog to the office, it's important that your colleagues are aware of some of the potential challenges.

Dogs of all ages can smell, shed hair, bark, and get up to mischief if bored. They can arrive with mucky paws or slobbery faces. They can roll in something vile on their way into work or on their lunchtime walk. They can have good days and bad days. They can growl if they feel threatened.

Are your colleagues prepared for this? Being able to express doubts they may have in advance of any agreement being made is vital, as is knowing that there is a process for discussing issues that may arise. I have had clients who took their dogs to work where colleagues have gone straight to HR with issues, rather than to the dog owner in the first instance, resulting in the imposition of harsh restrictions for the dog, such as being kept outside, or no longer being allowed in the office at all. If the concerns had been highlighted to the owners, they may have been able to resolve them. You may want to periodically check-in with your colleagues to allow you to nip any problems in the bud.

Planning the practicalities together

Once you have agreement in theory, it may be beneficial to discuss the practicality of having office dogs with your colleagues. This is a good way to suss out how willing they might be to shape their behaviour in order to accommodate the dog.

The post-walk look!

Some points you might want to consider –

? To which areas will the dog have access?

? Are other staff members willing to move items out of the dog's reach that they don't want him to have access to?

? If a behaviour becomes problematic, are colleagues willing to take a united approach as decided by the dog's owner (eg if the dog starts jumping up at people, will everyone agree to turn their backs? If the dog is begging for food, will everyone agree not to reward the behaviour?)

? If issues with the dog arise, will colleagues raise it with the dog's owner first?

Feedback

Try keeping any feedback anonymous. People who are uncomfortable with dogs may fear hostility from their dog-loving counterparts if they openly oppose anything to do with having dogs in the office. However, it is much better to know of any objections in advance: a compromise might be achievable.

You could start by sending around a questionnaire asking for colleagues' views about having dogs at work.

For any other concerns which may arise over time, you could provide a box in a discreet location where feedback can be left.

It is much better that your colleagues feel able to convey their concerns to you rather than going to management or HR, who may feel they have no choice but to terminate the dog-friendly arrangement.

? Are there any behaviours that would be really problematic, and represent a deal-breaker?

? Is there a policy for introducing new dogs?

Introducing new dogs

What if your dog is such a hit that other people in the office want to start bringing in their dogs, too? While dogs are inherently social creatures who enjoy the company of their own kind, putting dogs who don't know each other together in the workplace without careful introduction can be stressful and potentially problematic. As with everything else, devoting time and planning to the introductions will pay dividends in the long run. Agreeing in advance the procedure for bringing additional dogs into

Bobby in serious mode.

Case study: Bobby

Whilst running puppy classes in London, I had the pleasure of working with Mary and her pride and joy, Bobby, a 14-week-old Miniature Dachshund.

Mary is the kind of dog owner I love to meet. She had held off getting a puppy until she was sure she could meet all of his needs. She understood that a puppy couldn't be left at home alone while she went to work each day, so she had consulted with her workmates and boss, and had acquired Bobby on the understanding that he could come to work with her. Everyone was very enthusiastic at the thought of having a puppy at work ...

However, as anyone who has reared a puppy can attest, the reality of rearing a peeing, pooing, nipping, mischievous ball of fluff is not without its problems. Things got off to a good start in the office with Bobby, and everybody loved him. By the time he was five months old, however, the cracks had begun to show. Bobby was being a typical five-month-old dog; getting up to the usual mischief. He raided handbags left on the floor, and ran around the office. If he was crated to prevent behaviour like this, he barked. He barked at people coming into the office, and he barked at noises. Of course, Mary had strategies to deal with this behaviour: Bobby had things to chew, a snuffle mat to sniff around in, and regular breaks ... until the introduction of a rule that Bobby could eat food from his bowl only, lest mice be encouraged. Mary's best laid plans were falling apart ... The situation was becoming stressful for everyone involved, and Mary had to drastically reduce how often she took Bobby into the office.

Now an adult dog, Bobby is much better able to settle at work, and goes to the office on quieter days, happy to relax by Mary's desk. Mary is able to work from home two days a week, has a friend look after Bobby one day a week, and he goes to doggy daycare for the remaining two days.

In hindsight, Mary believes that taking Bobby into the office as a puppy was not the best idea, and that had she put other dog care arrangements in place until he was older, and gradually habituated him to the office, he would have been better equipped to manage the office environment, and able to go in every day as a result.

the equation can avoid arguments and misunderstandings should the situation arise.

Whenever introducing new dogs, doing so in a calm way, on neutral territory, and setting up the dogs for success, is always your best bet. If a colleague is planning to bring their dog to work, see if you can arrange to meet beforehand. Bringing the dogs together on a calm, on-lead walk, and allowing them to get to know each other slowly, will help set the scene for a harmonious life together at work.

Once everyone is friends, peace can reign in a multi-dog office! (Courtesy Lea Jochmann)

When taking them both to work for the first time, ensuring they have plenty of space between each other until you have established whether they get on is important. Using barriers so they are not constantly in each other's line of sight can be useful here, and bringing one dog in for half days initially can help prevent the situation from being too tiring or overwhelming.

If the dogs do not get on, what then? Is there sufficient space that both dogs can be kept in different rooms? Can a plan be made that they 'job share,' with one dog coming in on certain days or times and the other coming in on different days or times? Will one dog have to stop coming in? If so, whose dog will get priority? The dog who's been there longest? Or the dog belonging to the most senior person? Or will both dogs have to stay at home?

There are no right answers to these questions, but thrashing out these things in advance can prevent problems down the line.

Employees' perspectives

I've been busy getting anecdotes from dog owners who take their dogs to work, and those who work in dog-friendly offices. Staff at Kurgo Massachusetts shared their accounts of the funny things that can happen with a dog in the office, as well as the advantages and challenges of doing so.

On funny things that happen –

Here's a funny thing that sometimes happens when Clover is around. Sometimes I'll be working, clicking around with the mouse, and suddenly become aware that I'm playing tug-of-war with Clover, the Chocolate Lab. She has a way of sidling up with a toy and placing it in my free hand while I'm distracted. Even when I give the game my full attention, she always wins – she's strong as well as clever.
Elizabeth F (Operations)

Eevee peeing on the grass carpet every morning at 9am ... Clover pooping in Gordie's office on Lisa's first week at Kurgo ... Gus peeing on puppy Josie ... pretty much all of them revolve around going to the bathroom.
Mark M (Sales)

We often will bring in 'guest dogs' for photoshoots. One time, I brought in my friend's Lab. Not being familiar with the office, I took him for a walk so he could pee and poop before taking him in. That done, I took him upstairs, where he proceeded to run the entire length of the office peeing the whole time – so much for good intentions!
Catherine P (Marketing)

One day I was so excited about my lunch, I was so hungry and it was a delicious grilled chicken sandwich (I can still smell it). I got up from my desk to wash my hands, and when I got back my sandwich was gone. Initially I thought one of my co-workers was playing a trick on me, but I quickly realized that Yogi [office dog] had taken the entire sandwich off my desk and quickly devoured it before I got back. I was beside myself. Everyone thought it was pretty funny ... except me. I ended up scrounging crackers from the breakroom and bitterly ate them for lunch
Jodie C (Sales)

On the benefits of having dogs in the office –

There are *only* benefits! I love dogs, and I enjoy how some just randomly come visit me inside my cubicle on a daily basis, give me kisses, and leave.
Chandni L (Marketing)

One benefit is that you think a lot harder about getting a dog – and what kind of dog. I lost my Chocolate Lab about a year before starting at Kurgo. My initial instinct was to run out and get another dog, but having dogs around allowed me to take some time to decide if I wanted another dog, and what I was looking for: the bonus is that I got my dog fix nearly every day.
Catherine P (Marketing)

It's always fun to see a happy little pack of dogs running around and playing in the office. It makes you stop and get out of your head for a while. They offer the kind of distraction that is welcome when things get challenging.
Jodie C (Sales)

I think the dogs provide balance and happiness in the workplace. We spend so much time using the rational parts of our brains and staring at screens ... taking a little break to give a dog a scratch or watch a group of them goof around is a great antidote.
Elizabeth F (Operations)

Additional walks for both me and Gus ... no guilt about leaving Gus home all day ... excellent distraction when work gets overwhelming ... if you drop food on the floor at work, a dog will make cleaning it up much easier ... visitors to the office are usually pleasantly surprised to be greeted by 3 or 4 dogs looking for a treat.
Mark M (Sales)

I think one of the best benefits has been getting outside during the day to walk the dogs with co-workers. Sometimes it is just a couple of people; sometimes a group. But it's always nice to get to know the people that you work with in a more personal way.
Catherine P (Marketing)

And on the challenges –

Picking chewed paper scraps off the floor (hopefully nothing important, like a cheque)!
June P (Accounting)

Company lunches with dogs running around and begging for food ... dogs playing too rough/loud ... unauthorized Product Testing (dogs eating harnesses, bowls) ... dog hair everywhere.
Mark M (Sales)

Well, they are dogs. They do dog things: get in the trash, the puppies tend to chew anything that is in their sight, they have accidents from time to time, jump and bark at strangers ... but all these things are not so unexpected.
Jodie C (Sales)

Just when I wear black pants and pet a beige dog! Also the occasional slobber is less than pleasant for us non-dog folks!
Lori D (Sales)

There are always challenges to having your dog in the office. I have a puppy, and when she was really young, I had to take her out all the time. Then, as she got older and had more freedom, there is the constant supervision that she needs: she is constantly getting into people's garbage so the reality is that, some days, you simply aren't as productive with your dog in the office.
Catherine P (Marketing)

Canine communication skills

We all know that communication is key to cooperation and understanding in the workplace. Although we don't always recognise it, dogs are superb communicators. Ensuring that we make our intentions clear to them, and that we can understand what they are communicating to us, can avoid misunderstandings and conflict, so cluing up your work colleagues about canine communication can help things run smoothly in the office.

Things our dogs do to communicate

Dogs often do these things when stressed or when trying to diffuse tension or communicate peaceful intent

- Yawning
- Looking away
- Lip licking
- Sniffing the ground
- Freezing

There are many other calming signals that you can read about in Turid Rugaas' book *Calming Signs: on Talking Terms with Dogs*

Things we do that dogs find threatening or unpleasant

- Approach head on: approaching in a curve is much more polite
- Bending over them: crouching down to the side is better
- Head patting/side slapping: stroking on the side of the dog's neck or body is less threatening
- Direct eye contact/staring: can be perceived as hostile, so looking away and blinking can help a dog feel less under threat

Things we can do to help our dogs

- Curving: approach in a curve, and allow him to approach other people and dogs in a curve
- Splitting: standing in-between him and things he could find threatening will help your dog feel safe
- Hand signal: using the hand signal can let your dog know that he doesn't need to worry about whatever is happening/about to happen (see Chapter 5)

Example of a dog showing calming signs. (Courtesy Ali Souza)

In this photo, I am reaching over Leo, a dog I knew quite well. It's clear he's not comfortable. Look at his body language –

- *he looks away*
- *he blinks*
- *he licks his lips*
- *his ears are back*
- *his paw is raised*

Despite the fact that I am very familiar with all of these signals, I saw none of them at the time, and was shocked by my own lack of awareness. It was a very valuable lesson to me: even when you know a dog well, you must still pay attention to what he is saying to you, and not presume consent!

For example, it may be possible to put up posters providing basic information about canine communication in communal areas for staff members to read, or perhaps a doggy pack could be distributed to all members of staff containing some of this information. It has been my experience that people are usually really interested to learn how dogs communicate.

Getting other people involved in dog walking or toilet breaks

If you're lucky, some of your colleagues will take an interest in your dog, and may even wish to help you out by taking him for a walk or a toilet break, should you be tied up with something else. If you're happy with this and think that your dog will be agreeable, it's worth ensuring that anyone who wants to walk your dog undergoes some training first, otherwise, a well-intentioned colleague could inadvertently cause your dog stress or upset, perhaps by forcing encounters with other people or dogs, by having the leash too tight, or playing inappropriate games, etc.

He may also need company when you're required at meetings or out of the office for any other reason, especially in the early days. Again, being clear on what's required can prevent your dog having avoidable negative experiences, which could have a detrimental impact on his behaviour.

Poppy taking a rest.
(Courtesy Teressa McDonald)

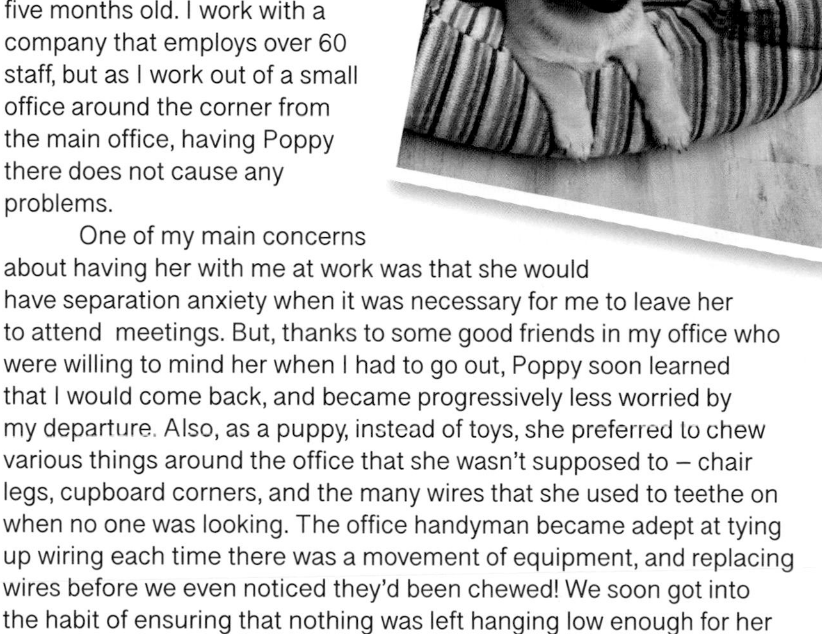

Case study: Poppy

I began taking Poppy (a Jug: Jack Russell crossed with a Pug) into work when she was about five months old. I work with a company that employs over 60 staff, but as I work out of a small office around the corner from the main office, having Poppy there does not cause any problems.

One of my main concerns about having her with me at work was that she would have separation anxiety when it was necessary for me to leave her to attend meetings. But, thanks to some good friends in my office who were willing to mind her when I had to go out, Poppy soon learned that I would come back, and became progressively less worried by my departure. Also, as a puppy, instead of toys, she preferred to chew various things around the office that she wasn't supposed to – chair legs, cupboard corners, and the many wires that she used to teethe on when no one was looking. The office handyman became adept at tying up wiring each time there was a movement of equipment, and replacing wires before we even noticed they'd been chewed! We soon got into the habit of ensuring that nothing was left hanging low enough for her to reach, and we all developed eyes in the back of our heads and keen hearing to avert the next bit of mischief. There was the occasional toilet-training accident, but these were mainly due to excitement.

Poppy has settled into the routine very quickly: a short walk before the hour-long drive to the office, where she immediately snuggles down for a sleep. Her bed is under a desk next to me, as we find that she settles much more easily if she can see me. At least once a day, she will ask to be picked up and likes to lie out on the desk! She also has a tendency to lie out behind people's chairs so we have all become used to looking before we move backward. Food is put down for her, but she doesn't usually eat it until about 11am. If she needs to go out, she'll let me know by jumping up at me, and I'll take her out for a walk in the local churchyard. If I am in a meeting when she needs to go out, there is always a colleague available to step into the breach. At lunchtime, we usually go for a walk around the town, where she is becoming well-

continued overleaf

known. There are also some dog-friendly eateries nearby, which we can use whenever there is a work celebration, meaning that Poppy can join in.

I am a solicitor and Director of Legal Services at a national estate planning company: a role with considerable responsibility, and one which can be very stressful. I have found that since I have been taking Poppy to work my stress levels have reduced and my blood pressure is lower than it used to be, too. The fact that I have to take her for walks means that I am away from my desk at lunchtime getting some exercise and fresh air, even if it's raining! Other staff also find that when things are getting on top of them or they have had a bad day, a visit from Poppy always lifts their mood. When we visit the main office, she will trot around and say hello to everyone. She is a real little charmer, and everyone who meets her falls in love with her.

We do put notices on doors: as it is a shared office there are often new people visiting who are unaware of her presence. The notices advise people to enter quickly and shut the door behind them!

Although taking Poppy into work hasn't been without its challenges, I would really recommend anyone to do the same, should the opportunity arise.

Teressa M
England

Reminders, signs, flyers, pop-up talks

Taking your dog into work has the potential to be great for you, your dog, and, indeed, your colleagues! It's also a good opportunity to educate people about dogs and their needs, and how to prioritise their welfare. People who are not used to dogs, or people whose way of interacting with dogs is at odds with your own, may well benefit from reminders about how to be around dogs.

For example, placing signs around the office can help remind others of how noise-sensitive dogs are; if your dog is nervous of strange people, or if your dog is in the process of training. Please see some examples you could use in Appendix A.

Occasionally having a dog trainer or vet come into the office to give short informative talks about dogs – at lunchtime, say – can also help colleagues feel more on board and included. I've done talks in dog-friendly offices in Dublin, and they've been very popular. You can find a list of members of the Pet Dog Trainers of Europe (PDTE) in your country on the PDTE website (https://www.pdte.eu/).

Chapter 2

Meeting your dog's needs

Understanding our dog's needs is imperative if we are to live (and work!) in harmony with them. A dog whose needs are being met is much less likely to be stressed ... and a dog who is not stressed is going to be less likely to exhibit behavioural problems, and be in a much better position to learn and understand what we want from them ... and a dog who can learn what we want from them, is going to do a lot better in the office environment!

Much like ourselves, dogs have a number of needs that must be met in order to survive and flourish. Some of these are core needs, without which the dog would be unable to survive. Others, while not crucial to their survival, play an important role in ensuring the dog lives a happy, fulfilled life.

As part of my research for this book, I undertook some qualitative research with a view to getting a detailed picture of what life in the workplace looked like for our dogs. The results were really interesting, but one thing that struck me was the fact that the routines of many of the dogs involved weren't set up in such a way that ensured their needs were being met. For example, most of the dogs were not getting enough sleep.

Sleep

Dogs spend only 10% of their sleeping time in REM sleep, compared to the 25% that people spend in REM sleep, which may account for why dogs need so much more sleep than we do. The general consensus is that dogs require 14-18 hours sleep a day (with puppies needing up to 20 hours, and elderly dogs also sleeping more than their younger counterparts), but a study on stress in dogs found that those who had 17 hours sleep or more a day were significantly less stressed than dogs who had fewer hours sleep. Dogs naturally get about 40% of their sleep requirement during the day.

So if your dog goes to work with you, it's important to ensure he has a safe, quiet place to sleep, and is not disturbed when sleeping. Providing a number of beds in various spots can ensure your dog will always find somewhere cosy to sleep! Dogs sleep polyphasically (in multiple blocks), so they often get up, mooch around for a bit, and then resettle somewhere new.

Bedding

Dogs spend so much time sleeping, investing in a good bed is really worth while!

They have different preferences with regard to beds, so choose something that works for your dog. Dogs with back or neck problems might appreciate something with sides they can lean into, or with cushions they can use to relieve pressure on their necks. Those with thin coats might prefer something cosy with added blankets.

A comfortable bed is essential for good sleep.

Food

Dogs need to eat at regular enough intervals to maintain a healthy blood sugar level. Hunger affects the brain, and has an impact on behaviour, mood, and learning ability. A hungry dog does not make a good office companion, so when you're packing your own lunch, spare a thought for Fido: including something food-based for your dog to chew, or the makings of a treat search, can provide diversion and enrichment, as well as staving off any hunger-induced behavioural problems.

It has become popular for owners who are training their dogs to use their daily food allowance throughout the day as rewards for good behaviour, working on the assumption that a hungry dog will work for their food. However, if a dog is forced to constantly be on alert to 'earn' a basic daily need, they will not be relaxed, and can become really food-obsessed. It is much better to give your dog his daily meals as normal and to use tasty lean extras (like chicken) as required for training. Alternatively, give him slightly less in his meals and hold back a small amount for training.

Steph's top tips for feeding your dog

* Ensure your dog has enough food regularly
* Feed a high quality food with real, identifiable ingredients. I try to feed a fresh diet (raw or cooked), but regardless of what you choose to feed your dog, watch out for nasty colours, additives, sugars etc, that can affect behaviour
* If your dog has weight problems but is still hungry, supplementing his diet with vegetables and lean protein can help
* Dry food takes a long time to expand in the stomach and make your dog feel full. Feeding a fresh or wet food can help your dog feel fuller, quicker!

Water

Your dog needs constant access to fresh water. Dehydration can cause serious complications, so do ensure he has access to water at all times when in the office.

Elimination

It's normal for dogs to pee 7-15 times a day (although puppies seem to go more often!). Dogs are naturally clean animals who will avoid soiling their living areas where possible, and many seem to quickly learn to extend this to most indoor areas. It is therefore quite unlikely that a toilet-trained dog will relieve himself in your office. However, needing to go to the toilet and not being able to is very stressful for dogs (and indeed, people!). Make sure you give your dog plenty of opportunities for toilet breaks, especially if you notice he's been eating or drinking, or is mooching around looking

TOP TIP!

If you are toilet training your dog and find it hard to predict when he'll need to go to the toilet when he has constant access to water, try offering him food with a high moisture content.

If he is getting a lot of water with his main meals, he is less likely to 'graze' on his water throughout the day.

Water should still be available throughout the day, of course.

Did you know?

As well as after food and drink, dogs often need to go to the toilet after any excitement. If you've just been playing with your dog, it might be a good idea to get him out of the office soon after!

Peeing more frequently than normal can be a sign of stress in your dog, and possibly illness such as diabetes.

anxious. This is also a good excuse to stretch your legs and return to work refreshed!

Social contact

Social contact is as important for a dog's health and well-being as are his physical requirements. Many dogs really struggle with being left alone while their owners go to work each day, and separation anxiety is a problem that I frequently encounter with my clients' dogs. One of the greatest benefits of being able to take your dog to work is that he won't be left alone at home, which can make a huge difference to his quality of life.

The difficulty in this regard may be that a dog at work can be overwhelmed by too much social contact! While company is very important to dogs, they often interact with each other differently to how we interact with them. Frequently having people interact with them in ways they don't necessarily enjoy (full-on approaches, bending over them, patting their heads, patting their sides) can be stressful for a dog (see *Canine communication skills* page 22).

Being at work can be socially rewarding for dogs, but to prevent him from experiencing stressful encounters, providing colleagues with information on canine communication, and stepping in if your dog is feeling uncomfortable, is a must!

Mental stimulation

In the wild, a dog would have important jobs to do each day, such as finding food, establishing safe places to hang out, managing interactions with other dogs, and protecting their young. All of these objectives require use of their brain, and our dogs have pretty good brains if we only give them the chance to use them!

Mental stimulation is really important to our dogs' quality of life, and one of the best ways to provide this is by giving them ways to use their nose. As sight-centred humans, it's easy to forget how

A Papillon puppy using his nose to track sausages!

nose-centred our dogs' existences are. I'm always encouraging clients to allow their dogs the opportunity to use their snouts more, and preaching the benefits of olfactory enrichment!

You could take an interactive toy into the office, or scatter some treats for your dog to find, or simply ensure that when you take him out for breaks that you allow him to have a good old sniff.

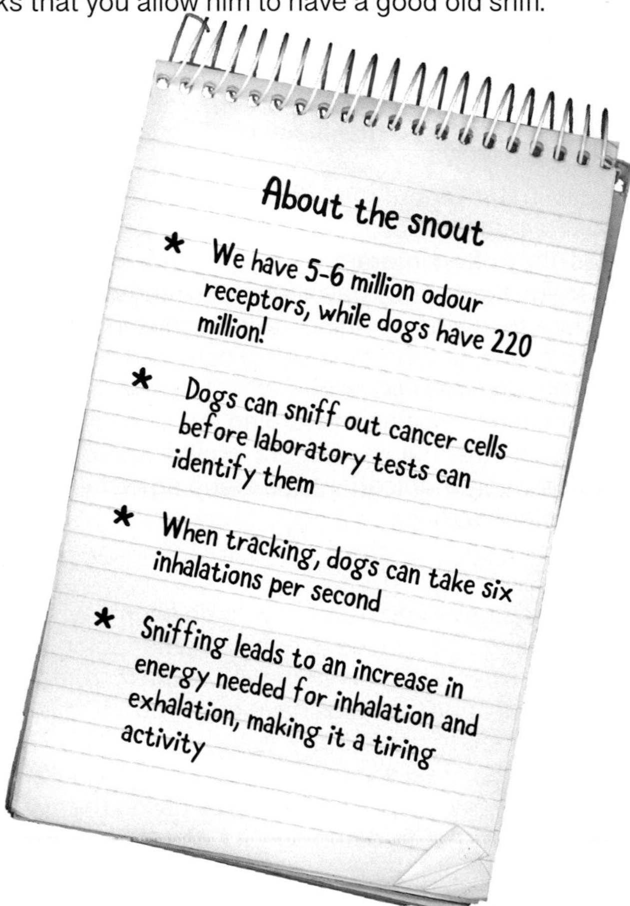

Sniffing is very tiring, and when using his nose, a dog's pulse rate drops, which helps create a tired, relaxed animal, ready to chill out when you return to the office

Choice

For lots of dogs, their entire lives are micro-managed. We decide where they sleep, what they eat and when, who they see and when, where they go and when, the speed at which they walk ... even where and when they can go to the toilet! Dogs who aren't willing to comply at all times are often labelled stubborn or wilful.

There are many reasons why a dog might not always want to do what is asked of him. He may be scared, or in pain, stiff or tired. He might not understand what is required, or why, and may decide that it's better not to comply. Imagine what it must feel like to always be expected – or even forced – to do as you're told. Our dogs may not always be able to convey to us why they can't or won't do what we're asking, but we can give them the opportunity to choose ... and we can respect those choices.

Giving your dog choices has a whole range of benefits –

✔ It encourages him to think before acting. Dogs have evolved to become one of the most successful creatures on earth, which would not have happened if they were unable to think and make good decisions! But often, we don't encourage them to think or take responsibility for themselves; instead, misguidedly encouraging impulsive behaviours like repetitively tearing after a ball

A somewhat unconventional choice of resting place!
(Courtesy Teressa McDonald)

Some ideas for doggy choices

* Where to go on walks: let your dog lead the way: it might surprise you!
* Provide a number of beds so your dog can choose where to sleep
* Offer a choice of treats. This is a good way to ascertain the current favourite
* Let your dog choose who to interact with. If he doesn't seem keen to say hello to a person or dog who wishes to greet him, make your excuses and move on. A lot of dogs don't like being touched by strangers, any more than we do!

✔ It makes him feel safer. Having choices about our life – and therefore being able to predict what's going to happen – brings with it a sense of security; having no control at all over our life is frightening. Dogs who are frightened will not be calm and relaxed office companions!

✔ It builds confidence. If a dog thinks about something, makes a choice, and sees a good result, this will naturally boost his confidence

✔ Having choice is a crucial factor in overcoming fear

If you're going to be taking your dog to the office, one of the most important choices to offer him is the choice to opt out if he wants to. If your dog seems reluctant to come along to the office, have you an alternative arrangement? Have you someone who can come in and let him out for a toilet break, or take him for a walk? Signs that your dog is not keen on office life include laying down when you try to get him ready to go; looking away, or walking off. Forcing him to go to the office when he clearly doesn't want to can lead to problems, as he's more likely to become stressed if forced to be somewhere he doesn't want to be.

Are there areas in your office that your dog simply doesn't like? Perhaps the stairs up to the canteen are difficult or frightening for him; maybe the floors in the hall cause him to slip and hurt his joints; maybe the room across the way is too noisy; or maybe he finds somebody who works in there frightening. If your dog doesn't want to be somewhere, there's probably a good reason why, even if we can't figure out what it is, and signs of this include him hanging back, looking away, licking his lips, or engaging in a displacement behaviour such as intently sniffing the ground or fiddling about and 'acting silly.'

Freedom of movement

Research increasingly confirms the damage that a sedentary lifestyle causes in us, with one study suggesting it poses a greater threat to our health than cholesterol or high blood pressure. Remaining sedentary for hours can cause a variety of health problems: joint and muscular pain, depression and anxiety, and even premature death. Less research has been done on dogs in this regard, but it stands to reason that, in the same way, inhibiting their movement for long periods of time can have detrimental consequences for canine health.

One of the biggest causes of inhibited movement in dogs is the crate, which I strongly urge people to avoid using at home and in the office. As well as the physical impact of inhibiting movement, keeping a dog in a cage for hours at a time can have many detrimental behavioural effects.

Rather than keeping your dog in a cage in the office, promoting sensible behaviour, providing sound outlets, and teaching him how to relax (see *hand signal* pages 62-64, and *calming signals* page 24) will allow him freedom of movement without being a nuisance to anyone in the office.

If you do need to create some sort of barrier, using dog/baby gates to section off areas can be a good alternative. Dogs often find these less distressing than being confined behind a door as they can still keep an eye on things. Cheaper, home-made alternatives can be just as effective: a plywood or polystyrene sheet might work, or some other sort of makeshift barrier.

The objective here is not to lock away your dog, but rather to create a space for you both by your desk, or in your corner of the office, so that you are between your dog and the door. This can reassure your dog that you are taking responsibility for the door, and anyone who should come through it, and help prevent any door-guarding issues arising. The space you create should, of course, still allow your dog plenty of room to move around.

Reasons to avoid crating

- ✗ It can increase frustration and lead to excessive biting and mouthing in puppies
- ✗ It increases anxiety
- ✗ It can negatively affect the social behaviour of the dog
- ✗ The dog can become shut down, and even reliant on the cage as a coping mechanism
- ✗ Although there are no restrictions on caging a pet dog in the UK or Ireland, such is the perceived detriment to a dog's welfare, in some countries it is illegal to crate a dog other than for specific purposes (such as travelling) and even then they must be walked every 3 to 4 hours

Chapter 3

Stressors

Too much stress is the primary cause of many of the behavioural problems I encounter in dogs. Stress in dogs is a rather interesting topic, as we usually associate stress with negative experiences. The first thing to remember about stress is that, physiologically, 'good' stress and 'bad' stress have the exact same impact on the body.

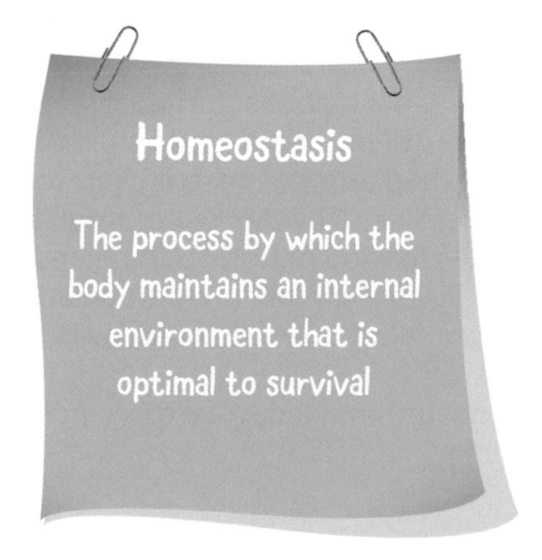

Stress occurs when the body enters a 'fight or flight' state as a result of danger or pain, or perceived danger or pain, or when the body needs to prepare for some sort of action. As the body prepares for this, it gears up those of its functions that will be of use in such a situation, and switches off the 'house-keeping' functions not necessary for immediate survival. The body is designed to enter this alert state occasionally, and then return to a state of calm in which homeostasis can occur. Problems arise, however, when the body spends too much time in this aroused state, as there is not enough time spent in 'house-keeping' mode. As a result, the body cannot maintain a state of homeostasis, and becomes vulnerable to a host of problems .

The adverse effects of stress on the body include –

- ☹ increased heart rate
- ☹ release of the anti-diuretic hormone ADH, resulting in the need to urinate (the body's way of jettisoning excess weight in preparation for action)
- ☹ impact on the immune system, resulting in illness, or even auto-immune disorders in some cases
- ☹ pain is not felt so acutely as a result of adrenaline in the system, making injury more likely
- ☹ because the body is primed for action, the dog is more likely to react to stimuli (this could be other dogs, cyclists, joggers, cats, etc)
- ☹ gastro-intestinal upsets such as loose stools and vomiting
- ☹ reproductive disorders

Cortisol – the body's main stress hormone – is released in times of stress, and can cause extensive damage to the body. Cortisol is released at a slower rate than adrenaline, but stays in the system longer, which means that when stressful events occur frequently, cortisol levels can remain elevated for extended periods of time, resulting in cells in the body being killed. Cells in the brain are particularly susceptible to the effects of cortisol, which not only kills brain cells, but also inhibits the production of new ones.

So, how can we ensure that a dog's experience of the workplace is as stress-free as possible?

The journey

Your journey to work may take a little more planning with your dog in tow. Keeping the journey as stress-free as possible will ensure that your dog gets off to a nice calm start in the office!

Travelling by car

If you're planning to drive to work, it's important to ensure that your dog is comfortable in the car. If he's unused to travelling by car, gradually acclimatise him to this.

Perhaps start off by scattering some treats in the car, with the doors open (whilst it's stationary, of course!), so he can potter around the car at his ease, having a nice time. Follow this with a few very short trips; perhaps give him something nice to chew or a little puzzle to solve

A safety harness that attaches to the seat belt is essential for car travel. (Courtesy Jude Brooks)

Does your dog get car sick?

Car sickness is particularly common in puppies, which many grow out of. In the meantime ...

* Sitting in a doggy booster seat also allows him to see out, and keeps him secure at the same time
* Try giving him a little piece of ginger biscuit before you head off (ginger has anti-sickness properties)

to keep him absorbed. You should be able to build from here, going on slightly longer journeys each time.

In the interests of safety, always ensure your dog wears a well-fitting harness that can be attached to the seat belt, as in the photo above.

Travelling by foot

While this may well be the most pleasant way for a young, healthy dog to travel to work, there are still a couple of things to be aware of –

- ✔ Allow plenty of extra time. Letting your dog sniff en route will ensure he's arriving at work feeling calm and pleasantly tired. Rushing him along will be frustrating for him and you!

Taking plenty of time to sniff!
(Courtesy Harriet Alexander)

- ✔ Don't overdo it. If your dog is still a puppy, remember not to go beyond the recommended amount of exercise for his age. This is five minutes per month of life, once or twice a day. So, if your puppy is five months old, that's a maximum of two, 25-minute walks each day. Likewise, if yours is an older dog, make sure he's not struggling on the walk. A tired dog is not always a good dog: dogs who are over-tired tend to be restless, and find it difficult to settle

- ✔ Use the right equipment. A well-fitting harness and a long lead will ensure the walk is comfortable for your dog

Travelling by public transport

Our dogs are much more sensitive to sounds and smells than we are, and this, along with the uncomfortably crowded nature of many forms of public transport, could make your dog's journey rather stressful.

- ✔ If you need to travel by public transport, try and avoid the crowds by leaving earlier or later in the morning

- ✔ Protect your dog from unwelcome attention from fellow travellers/dogs

- ✔ In the summer, some forms of public transport may become too hot for your dog, especially in the case of puppies and older dogs whose ability to regulate their temperature is compromised. In this case, it may be more appropriate to leave your dog at home and arrange another form of care, or perhaps find an alternative mode of transport

Remember also that allowing a dog on buses or in taxis is often at the driver's discretion.

Off-peak train travel can be an interesting experience for your dog.

Case study: Pater

Pater, a nearly blind Lurcher currently living in foster care, was suffering from separation anxiety when left alone. His foster carer, Lea, works in a dog-friendly office, but taking Pater along was difficult without a car, as the journey across town could be overwhelming for him.

Lea got in touch with me to discuss her dilemma, and we came to the conclusion that Pater's distress when left alone was probably greater than his fear of the journey to the office, so we got to work thinking about how we could make this easier for him.

Lea put a number of contingencies in place to make the journey as stress-free as possible for Pater, including –

- ✔ Segmenting the walk so that he could get to know these before trying out the entire walk
- ✔ Ensuring that the first few times he made the journey, Lea's husband, Christoph, could be there to act as a barrier between Pater and people who came too close, and to help him with things he found difficult, such as stairs. Lea and Pater did not attempt the entire trip without this support until Pater's confidence had grown
- ✔ Planning a route that had as little traffic and as many green places as possible to facilitate a calm, sniffy walk to work
- ✔ Teaching Pater cues such as 'careful' to alert him if he was getting too close to things, and tapping him on the shoulder to help direct him when needed

With this plan in place, Pater was well able to cope with getting to the office! Once there, he has no problem settling so long as there's someone in the room with him. A highlight for Pater is the afternoon ritual that Lea has introduced, whereby Pater and his doggy office colleague get to choose a treat to have whilst their people are having their tea-break: a routine much enjoyed by them both!

Pater gets a lot of attention in the common areas of the office, and although he seems to handle this attention, Lea makes a conscious effort to keep people from touching him too much.

Lea tells me that Pater makes up for his lack of sight with his remaining senses! His ears prick up if someone opens a packet of crisps three offices down the hall, apparently, and he's currently enjoying simple nose games at home and in the office.

Being able to go to the office has really improved Pater's quality of life, and Lea has been surprised by how far he's come in such a short period of time, taking office life in his stride, and how well he managed without full eyesight.

I love Pater's story, and think it goes to show how resilient dogs are, and how well they can conquer disabilities given just a little extra support!

▲ *Lea has her colleagues well-trained: they're happy for Pater to potter around without surprising him by patting him.*

◀ *Afternoon tea.*

(Both images courtesy Lea Jochmann)

Noises

Our dogs have really amazing ears! As well as being four times more adept at hearing than our own, they also have the remarkable ability to drown out the sound of their own barking. Our dog's ears are equipped with flaps that cover their ear canals when they bark.

Sadly, the ear flaps do not work when phones ring, doors slam, or shredders operate. Imagine being subjected to all of the sounds in your office, but four times more loudly? It's definitely another potential stressor for your dog!

Obviously, not all of these things can be controlled, but perhaps you could –

- ✔ Reduce the volume of your phone's ring
- ✔ Ask colleagues to be mindful of your dog's presence
- ✔ Position your dog's bed in a nice quiet spot away from loud machinery

Interactions (too many; the wrong type)

Dogs are inherently social creatures, and most of them crave companionship and company – much like us. One of the really great things about being able to take your dog to work is that it means he's not isolated at home whilst you're at work.

However, sometimes the way we communicate, and the way our dogs communicate, can be at odds, and misunderstandings can occur.

We are all prone to doing things to our dogs that they can find inherently threatening. We pat them on their heads, lean over them, approach them head on, pick them up, and hug them, none of which is considered polite or appropriate in the canine world. Whilst our dogs might be accepting of us doing these things (and I know there are some out there who seem simply unable to get enough attention!), they can find it very unsettling when people they don't know do them.

Boredom

Boredom is another stressor our dogs may experience in the office. For many, staying still and in one place for 8 hours while we work is frustrating and boring. Dogs like to be involved, and they like to have things to do. If your dog is restless or whiny, and other causes have been ruled out, he might simply be bored.

Providing things for him to do is really important if he's to enjoy his time in the office (and not cause mischief!).

Here are my suggestions for suitable office environment diversion –

- ✔ Things to chew
- ✔ A snuffle mat or other activity mat where he can search for treats

A Scent N Snack mat keeps a little chap entertained.
(Courtesy Alison Rowbottom)

Penny's office stash of chews!

- ✔ A treat search in the immediate area
- ✔ Teaching him some jobs (see Chapter 5 *Useful skills to teach your office dog*)

Of course, at the other end of the spectrum, it's important that he gets enough rest, so be careful not to overdo it!

Penny looking for her afternoon snack ...

Case study: Penny

Penny is a rescue Bull Terrier cross from Dogs Trust Dublin, who's about four-and-a-half years old. Richard and Desmond, Penny's people, own an architectural practice in Dublin city centre. Aware that other businesses in the premises had office dogs, they chose Penny with a view to taking her to their office.

'We deliberately went for an older dog, as we wanted one who would be appropriate for the workplace.' Desmond told me. 'Because they knew she'd be coming to work with us, Dogs Trust did an office check rather than a home check, and brought along Penny to meet the staff.'

Desmond and Richard would not have gone ahead with the adoption if their staff had not been happy with having Penny at work, as they felt that leaving her home alone all day was not an option. Thankfully, all of the staff get on well with Penny, and think she improves the atmosphere at work, as well as acting as a distraction from the computer screen on occasion!

From a managerial perspective, Desmond tells me he has no concerns about the impact that having a dog in the office might have on productivity: after all, he says, we're all supposed to take breaks from the computer for the sake of our health and our eyes. He'd have no issues with allowing colleagues to bring their dog to the office so long as the two got on.

Desmond and Richard used to travel to work by Luas (tram/light rail system in Dublin), but, as dogs aren't

... and on a site visit, happily ensconced in 'her' hole!

(Both images courtesy Richard McLoughlin)

allowed on this, they now usually walk to work, which takes 15-20 minutes. On rainy days, they take a taxi, although occasionally have a problem finding a driver who's happy to take Penny.

Penny sometimes takes a little while to settle at work, but, once she does, she spends most of the day snoozing on her bed by the radiator or under a desk. Penny has her meals at home, but has plenty of chews and toys at work, and always insists on having a treat when her human colleagues are having coffee! At lunch, she goes out for a walk, and enjoys meeting people on the street.

Penny does bark when anyone comes to the door, but, as there are few callers, it's not a big problem. The only issue they've had is that Penny has been barred from a coffee shop for barking at the owner, who was staring at her!

Occasionally, Penny goes on site visits, which are usually to rural areas. She really enjoys these, and will potter about whilst her people work. I just love the photo opposite of Penny relaxing in a nice hole on a site visit to disused church grounds!

Asked if he has any advice for business owners considering letting staff bring dogs to work, Desmond tells me that, as long as the dog and work environment are conducive to the arrangement, he'd definitely encourage it.

CHAPTER 4

Planning your dog's day at the office

Planning your dog's day in the office can be the difference between success and failure. This chapter will deal with some of the plans you can put in place to ensure your dog is happy, calm and coping!

A SUITABLE SPOT

Finding the most suitable location for your dog might take a little time and thought. In an ideal world, your dog should be able to choose where he would like to be, but this may not be possible. If you would like your dog to have a primary spot for resting in, it is important to choose somewhere he'll be as comfortable as possible. There are a few things to consider.

Proximity to you: This, perhaps, goes without saying, but it's likely your dog will want to be close to you. Is this possible? If you're based in an office, is there space for him near your desk?

Temperature: A dog's ability to regulate body temperature is more limited than ours. If he is too hot, he will tend to want to lie out in a cool spot on the floor. If too cold, he'll curl up. Consequently, placing your dog's bed in direct sunlight, beside a radiator, or next to an air-conditioning vent may deter him from using it! Temperature preferences vary dog-to-dog, with some always seeking nice,

Although she's free to move around, Sadie has a bed under her owner's desk.

sunny spots, and others seeking out cooler positions. Take your dog's preferences into consideration when choosing his primary location.

Noise: As mentioned previously, the superior hearing ability that canines have can mean they find some noises distressing, even though they may not bother us; it is therefore really important to find your dog a spot where noise is minimised. Can you turn down the volume of your phone's ring tone? Perhaps you can ensure you are away from noisy office machinery. Is your office somewhere people gather to chat and laugh or, even worse, argue and shout?

A good vantage point: Dogs are naturally curious, and curiosity is a great indicator of a happy dog. Many dogs will choose to rest where they can keep an eye on as many people and entry/exit points as possible.

Barriers: Alternatively, for some dogs, having a visual barrier in place can prevent him from being hyper-alert about things happening in the office.

This barrier keeps Huntley in a safe place with his person, whilst still allowing him to see what is going on. (Courtesy Jan Hugo Borg-Magnussen)

Busyness: How many people come in or out of your working space each day? Some dogs will thrive in a busy environment, but others will find this stressful, leaving their system flooded with stress hormones, and increasing the likelihood of their being hyperactive or reactive. If people are coming and going, encouraging them to greet your dog appropriately can reduce some of this stress (see *Gaining your colleagues' support*, page 14).

Things to do

Boredom is as stressful for dogs as it is for us, and a bored dog can become obstreperous and/or destructive. A good way to prevent boredom is to find suitable activities that will occupy your dog.

Chewing: This is a great activity for your dog. It is normal for dogs to chew on a daily basis, and doing so releases serotonin (a feel-good hormone). Keep a stash of chews for your dog, and either offer him one occasionally, or, if he can be trusted not to devour the whole lot at once, let him choose from these when he feels the urge to chew. I recommend natural, food-based chews. Some dogs enjoy cows' ears (less fatty than their better-known pig counterparts!), antlers, hooves, pizzles, etc. Raw bones are also appreciated by many dogs, but perhaps not as much by your colleagues, so are perhaps best kept for when your dog has access to an outdoor space.

Food puzzles: These are available in many pet shops and online – doggy puzzles, Kongs™, puzzle mats, snuffle mats, and many more activities to keep your dog engaged. My favourite is a snuffle mat, as it utilises a dog's nose and remains a challenge. Often, once puzzles have been mastered, they're no longer mentally challenging. Kongs™

How to treat search

* Chop treats into really small pieces, no bigger than half the size of your little finger nail
* Have lots and lots of these tiny pieces
* Find a suitable grassy spot, free of other dogs
* Scatter all of your treats into the grass in one fell swoop
* Say nothing; leave your dog in peace to find them

If your dog has never treat-searched before, drop a couple of treats on the ground in front of him first. It may take him a little time to build focus and get good at this. Don't worry if he doesn't stick at it for very long on the first few tries

can cause frustration if the dog can't get the food, so if you're using one, ensure they're challenging but also manageable!

Nose work: There are many nose games that you and your dog can play inside. One is simply an indoor treat search, where food is scattered on the floor for your dog to find. If not appropriate or permissible in your office, any outdoor space can be used for this purpose. Snuffle mats create a similar challenge, whilst containing the food in one place!

Hide-and-seek: Hiding a toy and having your dog find it can be great fun. Anne Lill Kvam's book, *The Canine Kingdom of Scent*, contains lots of great ideas for teaching your dog scent games. You could even teach him to retrieve lost items for your colleagues!

An adventure: Many of the dogs I've come across work with people whose job involves visiting other places on occasion. And for many dogs, one of their favourite things in the world is to visit new places and sniff new smells! If you have to travel somewhere for work, perhaps it would be possible to take along your dog?

Breaks

Your dog will need comfort breaks, so be sure to provide regular opportunities for him to get up and move around, and go to the toilet should he wish to. You might be able to take him for a short potter outside, or to another part of the building to meet a friend (human or canine!). This is a great reason for you to do the same: we're always

Molly sometimes relaxes in the car with the tailgate open whilst her dad views properties! *(Courtesy Kelly Hillis)*

being told how important it is to get up and move regularly if we have a sedentary job!

Lunchtime activities

How you structure your dog's lunch break requires serious thought. Many owners I've come across take their dog for a short, intense burst of activity at lunchtime: a game of fetch, or some boisterous play in the dog park. But care should be taken here, as engaging in this sort of fast, high-energy activity can leave you with a dog who is overwrought and adrenaline-fuelled – or sore and uncomfortable. Adrenaline remains in the system for many hours, so can affect your dog's behaviour long after the activity has ceased.

Appropriate lunchtime exercise

A slow, sniffy walk: Somewhere new, perhaps? Dogs love exploring unknown places, even if we can't see the attraction!

Treat search: Remember, sniffing is a lovely, calm way to tire your dog without getting him over-excited

A social walk with friends: Calm walks with doggy friends are a lovely experience for your dog. Even if they don't seem to be interacting with each other, they'll be pleasantly tired out afterwards

Nose games: Whether it's finding keys or some basic trailing, your dog will be tired and contented afterwards. Just don't do too much!

A treat search amongst the leaves!

A walk with friends.
(Courtesy Harriet Alexander)

This puppy is searching for pate that has been smeared on a tree – a 'treat tree' – another good way to engage his nose on your lunchtime stroll.

Resting in the sun.

A rest: If your office is a very busy place, going somewhere where your dog can simply lie down and relax quietly for a while might be your best option.

Inappropriate lunchtime exercise

Ball/frisbee/stick/squirrel chasing: This sort of activity repeatedly triggers the prey/chase response in dogs, resulting in the body being flooded with stress hormones such as adrenaline and cortisol. As a result, dogs are often quite wired afterwards, and quicker to react. If these activities take place regularly, the adrenal gland becomes enlarged and produces elevated stress hormones constantly. Sometimes, there is an initial 'gain' for the owner as the dog can be physically tired after intense exercise. However, when he recovers from the physical tiredness, the stress hormones will still be present, and undesirable behaviours can occur as a result.

Additionally, activities that flood the system with adrenaline can mean that pain is minimised, allowing the dog to do himself harm or exacerbate existing injuries. Even old or infirm dogs will sometimes seemingly 'forget' they have pain once a ball (or squirrel or cat!) appears, as their excitement and the adrenaline in their bodies minimises this.

However, once the adrenaline wears off they will surely pay the price for their exertions. It is also not unusual for otherwise healthy dogs to damage their cruciate ligaments during play like this, which often involves fast-starting, leaping, twisting, and sudden stopping.

Purely physical exercise such as jogging, running alongside a bike or walking quickly: Dogs will use up a lot more energy sniffing things and engaging with the world than they will doing purely physical exercise, and this type of exercise – which compels them to keep moving at the same pace and prohibits natural sniffing behaviour – can be stressful, and even dangerous, especially if the dog is on a lead alongside a moving bicycle.

Days off

Going to work every day might be too much for some dogs. If, occasionally, your dog doesn't seem keen to come along, respect his decision and have a back-up plan in place, such as a suitable dog sitter, or his staying with a neighbour.

Additionally, while there are indisputable advantages to having dogs in the workplace, it is an added responsibility for us: we may also benefit from work days when we don't have to worry about our dog.

All in a day's work

Overleaf are a couple of examples of how your dog's day at work might look. Note that the emphasis is on calming physical activities and mental stimulation, with lots of rest!

Your dog may find that the process of getting to work, being in work, and the various social interactions that this will require quite tiring, and will not need buckets of additional entertainment in addition to this.

Toilet breaks, although specifically marked on the examples, should be provided whenever required, and not necessarily to a schedule.

TIME	ACTIVITY
7.30am	Breakfast
8.00-8.20am	Nice, slow, sniffy walk
8.20-9.00am	Drive to work
9.00-11.00am	Rest
11.00am	Short toilet break
11.10am-1.00pm	Rest
1.00-1.30pm	Slow, sniffy walk or outdoor nose game such as a treat search or treat tree
1.30-4.00pm	Rest
4.00pm	Short toilet break
4.10-4.20pm	Visit friends in the office. Perhaps, as a little job for him to do, your dog could take them a pen, or a magazine?
4.20-5.00pm	Rest
5.00-5.40pm	Drive home

TIME	ACTIVITY
8.30am	Breakfast
9.00-9.15am	Nice, slow walk to train station
9.15-9.50am	Train journey to work: a little off-peak, so quieter, hopefully!
9.50-10.00am	Leisurely walk from train to office
10.00am-12.00pm	Rest
1.00- 1.30pm	Social walk with canine friends
1.30-4.00pm	Rest
4.00pm	Short toilet break (and perhaps a treat search if your dog is feeling energetic)
4.15-6.00pm	Rest
6.00-6.40pm	Journey home

Case study: Cookie

For many dogs, less is more when it comes to being an office dog, and this is especially true of older dogs, who often spend a lot more time sleeping than do their younger counterparts. However, that doesn't mean they can't enjoy a day in the office!

Cookie is an elderly Labrador who has been going to work with her person for the past few years. Cookie, as an older dog with arthritis, struggles to do much by way of physical exercise. Each day before work, she goes for a very short walk (300-500m/328-546yd), and is then carried to the car. She is driven to work, and has a another short stroll of around 200m (218yd) to get to the office. Once in the office, Cookie rests in her bed under her person's desk for five or six hours. At this point, she is carried downstairs for a short toilet break. After being carried back upstairs, she happily sleeps for another two hours before home-time. Cookie is carried downstairs again and walks the 200m to the car. Once she gets home she has dinner, another short walk, and then she's straight back to bed!

For Cookie, going to work means she doesn't have to be left home alone, and for most dogs, as social sleepers, being able to spend the day sleeping next to your person is far preferable to sleeping alone at home!

Cookie resting at work.
(Courtesy Lea Jochmann)

Equipment

As well as planning the journey and the day, having the right equipment to hand at the office can be a big help in ensuring all goes well. Obviously, individual dogs will have varying preferences and requirements, so the list below is intended as a guide only.

- ✔ A well-fitting harness and a long lead. I recommend harnesses for all dogs, and especially for safety reaons when travelling by car. It's important that the harness fits well, avoiding any pressure on the neck, ensuring that the shoulders are free of restriction, and allowing 5cm (1.9in) of clearance behind the front legs to avoid chaffing. Haqihana and Calming Signs make harnesses that meet these criteria.

  Collars can do untold damage to the delicate structure of the canine neck and its anatomy, from the muscles to the thyroid; the vertebrae and nerves. A harness that fits well will distribute pressure across the bony thorax, which is better able to absorb shock. Remember that a harness that is perfect for walking in, may not be perfect for lying down in, as the buckles can dig into your dog. Whilst a harness should be used for walks, toilet breaks, sniffing activities, or anything that requires a lead attachment, a soft house collar may be more suitable for indoor use

- ✔ Poo bags

- ✔ A comfortable bed, or, better still, beds, so that your dog has a choice of where to lie

- ✔ Things to do

- ✔ A water bowl and food bowl, and wipe-clean mat for these

- ✔ Snacks, treats and suitable items for chewing

- ✔ A towel if your dog is likely to get wet en route to work or on his lunchtime outing: there's nothing like the smell of wet dog to put people off an office dog!

- ✔ Clean up equipment: carpet cleaner, disinfectant, paper towels. Hopefully these won't be needed, but much better to be safe than sorry. Your dog could have a bug or an upset stomach, and accidents do happen! If they do, deal with them promptly to maintain your colleagues' support of a dog-friendly policy

A well-fitting harness is essential.

▶ *Molly waiting to jump aboard for the start of a working day ...*

▲ *... and taking a well-earned break by the sea.*
(Both images courtesy Kelly Hillis)

Case study: Molly

The life of an estate agent really works for Molly the German Shepherd, and every day she goes to work with her dad at his estate agency in Cork, Ireland.

The day begins with a drive to the office, where Molly takes up position at the receptionist's desk while her dad goes through the diary for the day, before making her way into the office. She has a choice of two beds here, but her favourite spot is usually at her dad's feet!

Molly sits in on meetings in the office, and in the afternoon goes on property visits so that her dad can measure-up the properties or show them to potential buyers. If the clients are amenable, she will go into the houses with him while he works, but, if not, the car door is left open so that she can relax and observe proceedings from there.

This is usually followed by a swim in the sea, and then Molly is dried and brushed before heading back to the office or home.

Sometimes there's even an ice-cream stop, and the two of them sit in the boot of the car with the door open eating their ice-creams!

What a delightful life for a dog!

Chapter 5

Useful skills to teach your office dog

The hand signal

Turid Rugaas is a proponent of using this hand signal in a multitude of situations. Dogs appear to have an innate understanding of the message we are trying to convey without ever being 'taught' it.

How to do it: Raise your hand in a 'stop' sign, elbow bent, hand relaxed, palm facing out.

When to use it: Any time you're going to move away from your dog; if your dog is begging; if your dog is trying to get something he shouldn't; if your dog is barking, and countless other situations. If in doubt, hand signal!

How it applies in the office: It's likely you're going to be moving around at work, and probably don't want your dog to follow you each time. Using the hand signal before you move will help reassure him that he doesn't need to become involved. Equally, if your dog is trying to stick his snout into someone's bag, or climb onto someone's lap, they can use the hand signal, and If your dog is barking, the hand signal can let him know that he does not need to be concerned if he's worried about something.

Agnes Vaelidalo, a Norwegian dog trainer, has carried out research into the effect on the pulse rates of dogs when the hand signal is used, and recorded this on video. In one recording when the dog's owner walks away from him without doing the hand signal, the dog's pulse rate rises by nearly 100%, from 88 to 150, whereas when she uses the hand signal, the dog's pulse rate rises to 100. This owner had never used the hand signal before.

The hand signal is much more effective than issuing verbal commands or pushing away the dog, as verbal/physical attention such as this can actually reward the dog's behaviour.

This hand signal is remarkably effective when used consistently.

Teaching your dog to be calm

This is the simplest cue in the world to teach, and one of the most useful, too.

How to do it: Find yourself somewhere comfortable to sit, and put some beds around for your dog to choose from. You can start off with your dog on a lead and harness so he doesn't wander off and play. Hold on to the lead and just sit perfectly still and perfectly silently, and wait for your dog to settle (depending on how relaxed or otherwise your dog is, this may take some time). Just wait.

Once he lies down and relaxes, say nothing; don't praise him or pet him, just continue to stay still for a while. Practise regularly so that your dog learns that once you sit down, he can sit down and relax, too. Once he can do it at home, you can start practising in gradually more challenging places. Eventually, whenever you sit down, your dog will just relax.

When to use it: Whenever nothing is happening and you want your dog to relax.

How it applies in the office: When you sit down, your dog will realise that nothing else is happening, and that he can relax. If you briefly get up, use the hand signal above to let your dog know that he doesn't need to come, too. This is also useful if you're waiting for, or sitting in, a bus or train, or travelling by car.

Go to

This is a bit of fun that can provide your dog with a useful job which he may well enjoy – and your colleagues are bound to be impressed, too!

How to do it: Find a helper for this one. You, your dog and your helper should walk together for a little while, then, ask your helper to hold onto your dog's harness whilst you walk a few steps away. Standing sideways, or crouching down (this will prevent you looking threatening), call your dog to you. At this point, the helper should let go, and the dog should come to you. You can give your dog a treat and lots of praise when he gets to you.

Now, you hold your dog's harness for a few seconds, and then ask him to 'go to [helper's name].' The helper should call your dog, and when he seems keen to go (the first time you're doing this your helper may need to show that they have a tasty treat!), release the harness and the helper should give the treat to the dog (and also praise him) when your dog reaches them.

Once again the helper holds your dog's harness, you move away, and the helper asks your dog to 'go to' you.

Over time, you could teach your dog the names of the people in your office, and you'll be able to send him to them. If your dog likes to carry things in his mouth, you can ask him to 'go to' with an item to deliver to your colleague.

How it applies in the office: This is a nice way for your dog to have something worthwhile to do. It can alleviate boredom, and also promote bonding between him and your colleagues. Who's not charmed by a gift from a dog?

Case study: Huntley

Huntley is a 6-year-old Collie, who's been going to work in service technology with his owner, Jan Hugo, in Oslo, Norway, for about a year. When Jan Hugo began working in his current role, he noticed that other staff members brought their dogs to work, so he started taking along Huntley, too.

Interestingly, a couple of Jan Hugo's colleagues are allergic to dogs but this hasn't caused any issues. One of them avoids Huntley's office, but is fine in the neighbouring offices, and the other, who likes animals and has animals of his own, simply takes medication, and regularly visits Huntley.

Huntley enjoys the social aspect of going to work, and likes to interact with his human colleagues. If the attention gets too much, Huntley just stops getting up when people come into the office, and they accept this, without putting him under pressure. Jan Hugo tells me that most of his colleagues like Huntley, and some simply love him!

Although there are other dogs around, they don't often meet, but, when they do, there are no problems.

The only problem they have encountered was that Huntley initially found it difficult to be contained in one room: something he was not accustomed to, but, because of the movement of machinery around the building, it's not safe for him to wander on his own. Jan Hugo overcame this particular difficulty by taking him out for a trip whenever he became restless. Initially, these trips were very frequent, but, as time passed, Huntley needed fewer trips out, and now settles very well. He has some interactive toys which Jan Hugo hides treats in for him, and is in fact so calm that Jan Hugo has been asked if he's been drugged! Needless to say, he has not: his relaxed nature and the fact that he leads a calm life have created an ideal office temperament.

Huntley relaxing.
(Courtesy Jan Hugo Borg-Magnussen)

continued overleaf

Huntley's routine is to have a very early morning walk in the forest for about 30 minutes, during which he has many messages from the local wildlife to smell, before the trip to work. The pair arrive at around 7am, and Huntley likes to have a treat on arrival. He's ready for another walk and his lunch by around 10.30am. He is extremely intolerant of any delay to this particular part of the day, and will stand up and let Jan Hugo know he is ready, if he is even a couple of minutes behind schedule!

Huntley is happy to relax in the office until they head home at around 3pm, when he has another walk in the forest.

Chapter 6
Troubleshooting

Barking

Dogs bark for lots of reasons – fear, frustration, excitement, guarding, etc. If your dog is barking at people who come into the office, it is likely to be fear or a desire to guard that is motivating him (although it is possible that frustration could be the cause if your dog is used to greeting people, and is prevented from doing so in the office).

If your dog is barking because he is frightened or trying to guard his space, reassure him by standing in-between him and whoever or whatever he's barking at. This is known as 'splitting' and is a behaviour that dogs will engage in themselves to break up tense situations between people, or when play has become too intense between two dogs.

When we 'split,' and stand between our dog and 'the threat' (which could be another person, another dog, or a frightening object), we convey to him that we are managing the threat, and that he can let go of that responsibility. It can also serve to break intense eye contact which can be perceived by our dog as an act of aggression.

It may be easier for a colleague with whom your dog is familiar to do this if they are in a better position to stand up and be a barrier (if your dog is in front of your desk, for instance, it could take you some time to get up and around to him). You (or your colleague) should stand close to the dog, facing whatever it is that he finds threatening, with hands spread by your side. Remain in this position until 'the threat' is gone, or your dog has relaxed and stopped barking. A video about splitting on www.dogpulse.org highlights how effective this is in reducing a dog's anxiety.

You can also try using the hand signal as discussed in Chapter 5 *Useful skills* ... Using visual blocks, such as a screen, say, so that your dog cannot stare at the door, can also help, although some dogs find it more worrying not being able to see whatever it is that is the problem.

Scolding or shushing your dog is unlikely to help and is best avoided. Turid Rugaas' book *Barking: The sound of a language* is a really good resource for dealing with the various types of barking you may encounter.

Your dog can't settle at work

A dog can find it hard to settle for a number of reasons, which may include –

- ☹ He's never learned to settle, or the unsettled behaviour has been inadvertently rewarded (any sort of contact – negative or positive, verbal, physical or visual – can serve as a reward). Try having regular calm sessions (as described in *Useful skills*) so that your dog has the chance to learn this valuable skill

- ☹ Dogs who have been over-exercised, or who are over-tired, can be restless and find it hard to settle. If this is the case, you may want to replace some of your dog's physical exercise with mental stimulation in the form of nose games or puzzles

- ☹ He is physically uncomfortable. This could be the result of pain or an illness, or due to environmental issues (the environment is too noisy; he doesn't have a safe, comfortable place in which to lie; he is too hot/cold, etc)

- ☹ He is stressed. Hyper-activity is a common symptom of stress. If your dog is stressed, ensuring his needs (as outlined in *Meeting your dog's needs*) are met, and he is taking part in appropriate activities is a good start

- ☹ He is bored. This is particularly common in younger dogs, and providing him with suitable things to chew, and mental stimulation, can help

Or, he may simply need a toilet break, water, or food!

It's just not working ...

Being in the office will not work for all dogs, and if, despite implementing the suggestions in this book, things aren't going well, and your dog does not seem to be enjoying the experience, it may simply be that the work environment is too much for him to cope with.

Reducing the time spent in the office might help in this case: maybe just half-days? Could someone collect your dog at lunchtime and take him home for the afternoon, perhaps? Or, could he be at home for

Pain

Pain in dogs can be hard to identify and diagnose, especially if it is muscular, as dogs hide pain very well.

The following can be indicators of pain in your dog –

* Panting when it's not hot
* faster than usual heart rate
* areas of heat or cold on his body
* stretching a lot (for instance, frequently doing the 'downward dog' position)
* fur that is not lying properly or is of a different texture. This can suggest an underlying muscular problem
* Change in movement, gait or posture

If you think your dog may be in pain, a visit to your vet is your first stop. You may wish to ask your vet about a referral to a canine massage therapist or physiotherapist the morning, then walked by a dog-walker who drops him back to your workplace for the afternoon? Are there days when a neighbour or family member could mind your dog instead of him going to the office?

Alternatively, not taking him to the office at all for a few weeks, and then gradually building the time he spends in the office over a period of weeks or months might help to habituate him to the new environment. This may be particularly pertinent with puppies, who, like young children, do not do well if expected to stay still with nothing to do for long periods of time.

Are there other things in your dog's life that might be stressing him? Dogs are subject to the build-up of stressors just as we are, and if your dog is constantly on the go or on the alert when not in the office, he might simply not have the energy to contend with the experience. Perhaps you need to review what else is going on in your dog's life, and embark on a doggy stress-reduction programme!

Your office may not be a suitable environment: if it's too noisy or busy for your dog, you may need to give up on the idea of having your dog at work, even if your company allows it. Are there other locations you could work from that may better suit your dog?

Epilogue

As mere mortals, we can often fall into the trap of believing that our dogs are very lucky to live with us, enjoying free bed and board, no necessity to work, and none of the human stressors that we encounter on a daily basis.

However, in reality, it is *we* who are lucky to have *them*.

Dogs have come in from the wild to share our lives, our sofas, and our hearts, and, in doing so, have sacrificed a life of autonomy and freedom. We owe to it to them to ensure their lives are as happy and fulfilling as possible.

If you have the opportunity to take your dog to work with you, it's important to strike a balance so that the experience enhances your dog's life rather than detracts from it. For many of us, work is the source of some degree of stress, and having our dogs there can alleviate this somewhat, as their very presence de-stresses us. But we must ensure that the experience is also a pleasant one for them, and I hope that my book has gone some way to showing how this can be achieved with relative ease.

Remember: plan ahead, and if it's not working for your dog, reconsider! Not all dogs will enjoy being office dogs, and for them, a dog walker or minder may be a better option.

For those who do enjoy the experience, though, the guidance provided here should help to ensure it remains that way.

Appendix

References and further reading

Books

- Rugaas, T, 2005. *On talking terms with dogs: Calming signals.* Dogwise Publishing

- Rugaas, T, 2007. *Barking: The Sound of a Language.* Dogwise Publishing

- Kvam, A L, 2011. *The Canine Kingdom of Scent.* Dogwise Publishing

- Hallgren, A, 2013. *Stress, anxiety and aggression in dogs.* Cadmos Publishing

- Sapolsky, R M, 2004. *Why zebras don't get ulcers: The acclaimed guide to stress, stress-related diseases, and coping* (now revised and updated). Holt paperbacks

- Scholz, M and Von Reinhardt, C, 2006. *Stress in Dogs: learn how dogs show stress and what you can do to help.* Dogwise Publishing

- Jensen, P ed, 2007. *The behavioural biology of dogs.* Cabi

- Nordengen, K, 2018. *Your Superstar Brain.* Piatkus Books

Websites

- Dogpulse.org (2018). The dog pulse project/Walk in a curve when you meet a dog! http://www.dogpulse.org

- Freedogz.be (2018). FreeDogz. http://www.freedogz.be/equipment/
- Washington Post (2018). Millennials are picking pets over people. https://www.washingtonpost.com/news/business/wp/2016/09/13/millennials-are-picking-petsover- people/?utm_term=.47df9a9485b3
- Inc.com (2018). But Is it Legal? Dogs in the Office. https://www.inc.com/chas-rampenthal/dogs-in-the-office-is-it-legal.html
- News.vcu.edu (2018). Benefits of taking Fido to work may not be far 'fetched.' https://www.news.vcu.edu/article/Benefits_of_Taking_Fido_to_Work_May_Not_Be_Far_Fetched
- Siop.org (2018). Canine Coworkers. http://www.siop.org/article_view.aspx?article=996

Papers

- Hall, S, Wright, H, McCune, S, Zulch, H and Mills, D, 2017. Perceptions of dogs in the workplace: the pros and the cons. Anthrozoos, 30(2), pp291-305
- Olsen, P E. 2015. See Spot run? The dogs in the workplace debate. Journal of Case Studies, 33(2), pp116-122
- Segerstrom, S C and Miller, G E, 2004. Psychological stress and the human immune system: a meta-analytic study of 30 years of inquiry. Psychological bulletin, 130(4), pp601
- Wilkin, C L, Fairlie, P and Ezzedeen, S R, 2016. Who let the dogs in? A look at pet-friendly workplaces. International Journal of Workplace Health Management, 9(1), pp96-109
- Barker, R T. Knisely, J S, Barker, S B, Cobb, R K and Schubert, C M, 2012. Preliminary investigation of employees' dog presence on stress and organizational perceptions. International Journal of Workplace Health Management 5(1), pp15-30
- Allen, K, Blascovich, J and Mendes, W B, 2002. Cardiovascular reactivity and the presence of pets, friends, and spouses: The truth about cats and dogs. Psychosomatic medicine, 64(5), pp727-739

- Friedmann, E, Thomas, S A, Cook, L K, Tsai, C C and Picot, S J, 2007. A friendly dog as potential moderator of cardiovascular response to speech in older hypertensives. Anthrozoos, 20(1), pp51-63

- Foreman, A M, Glenn, M K, Meade, B J and Wirth, O, 2017. Dogs in the workplace: a review of the benefits and potential challenges. International journal of environmental research and public health, 14(5), pp498

OFFICE DOG INSIDE

Please close the door behind you!

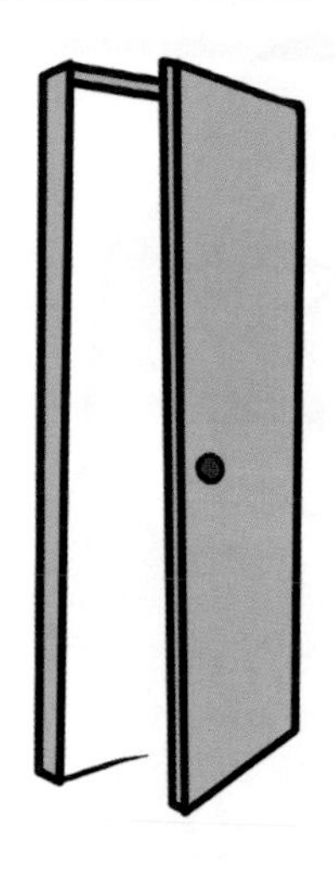

I'm a superb escape artist!

Please enter promptly and close the door behind you!

Office dogs: The Manual - A comprehensive guide to dogs in the workplace
© Hubble & Hattie and Stephanie Rousseau ISBN: 978-1-787113-81-7 2018

OFFICE DOG INSIDE

"If you'd like to say "Hello," please let me approach you!"

I'm a little bit nervous of new people, so if you're coming in please:

- **wait for me to approach you;**
- **look at me from the side rather than straight on (I'm shy!);**
- **if I approach you and you wish to say 'hi', come down to my level and stroke my side;**
- **if you need to approach where I'm sitting, approach in a curve.**

Thanks for your understanding!

Office dogs: The Manual - A comprehensive guide to dogs in the workplace
© Hubble & Hattie and Stephanie Rousseau ISBN: 978-1-787113-81-7 2018

Index

This unique book combines the joys of camping with the delights of walking your dog. A variety of campsites – all of which welcome dogs – located very close to footpaths and walking trails, provide the opportunity to explore the area, and truly appreciate the diverse environments found in Britian.

Paperback • 15.2x22.5cm • 248 pages • 146 colour images
• ISBN 978-1-787110-45-8 • £14.99*